The Parent to Parent Adding Wisdom Award honors products that entertain, teach, and inspire. Every product is reviewed by a committee at Parenttoparent.com as well as by a family. Past winners have included the Magic Tree House *series,* Scholastic Parent & Child Magazine, *PBS Kids, and Disney.com.*

2009 Parent to Parent Adding Wisdom Award for Humor
and a *ForeWord Magazine* Humor Book of the Year Finalist

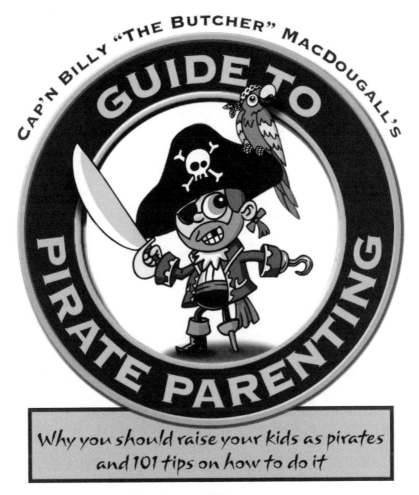

CAP'N BILLY "THE BUTCHER" MACDOUGALL'S
GUIDE TO
PIRATE PARENTING

Why you should raise your kids as pirates
and 101 tips on how to do it

TIM BETE

The award-winning parenting humor columnist and author of
In The Beginning...There Were No Diapers

Cold Tree Press
Nashville, Tennessee

A Trade Paperback Press

Publisher's Cataloging-in-Publication data

Bete, Tim.
    Cap'n Billy the Butcher Macdougall's guide to pirate parenting: why you should raise
your kids as pirates and 101 tips on how to do it / Tim Bete.
    p. cm.
    ISBN 978-1-58385-291-0
1. Parenting—Humor. 2. Parenthood—Humor. 3. Child rearing—Humor. 4. Parent and
child—Humor. 5. Pirates—Humor. I. Cap'n Billy the Butcher Macdougall's guide to pirate
parenting: why you should raise your kids as pirates and one hundred and one tips on how
to do it II. Title.

PN6231.P2 B55 2009
818/.5402 20
2009920987

*Cold Tree Press is an independent, trade paperback press committed to introducing fresh, exciting voices
to the reading public. It is our mission to take a chance on deserving authors and achieve the
highest quality when bring their words to the marketplace. We believe in the power of words and ideas
and strive to introduce readers to new, creative writers.*

www.coldtreepress.com

Published by Cold Tree Press, Nashville, Tennessee

*For information regarding permission, write to:
Cold Tree Press, 5560 Franklin Pike Circle, Suite 112, Brentwood, Tennessee 37027.*

Library of Congress Number: 2009920987

New Edition, 2009

*ISBN-13: 978-1-58385-291-0
ISBN-10: 1-58385-291-3*

Cap'n Billy's 100% Money-Back Guarantee

Captain Billy "The Butcher" MacDougall is so confident his advice will turn your child into a pirate, he guarantees results. If you follow the instructions in this book and your child does not become a pirate, Cap'n Billy will refund the full purchase price of this book.*

This guarantee assumes you have applied the principles in this book with your child for a period of 18 years. It also assumes you can find Cap'n Billy and that he remembers the guarantee. To claim a refund, you must bring your child to Cap'n Billy and let him decide if your child is really a pirate or not. Cap'n Billy reserves the right to make refunds in salt cod in lieu of cash, not that he plans to give any refunds.

Pronoun disclaimer: Some readers will notice that Cap'n Billy usually refers to pirates as men or boys. (e.g., "When your child is picking his nose, he is really 'digging for buried treasure.'") Cap'n Billy means no offense by this. (He's offensive about many things—this just doesn't happen to be one of them.) Cap'n Billy considered using "he or she" whenever referring to your child but found it as cumbersome as maneuvering a 50-foot ship through a coral reef in a dense fog. There is some basis for referring to pirates as men. The latest pirate census found that 94 percent of pirates are male, 4 percent are female, and 2 percent have appeared on the *Jerry Springer Show*.

Table of Contents

PART I:
Introduction

PART II:
Cap'n Billy "The Butcher" MacDougall's Guide to Pirate Parenting

CAP'N BILLY "THE BUTCHER" MACDOUGALL'S

GUIDE TO

PIRATE PARENTING

Why you should raise your kids as pirates
and 101 tips on how to do it

TIM BETE

Arrrr! Avast, ye landlubbers,
yer about to set sail with Cap'n Billy...

PART I:

Introduction

How I Met Cap'n Billy and Why You Should Raise Your Children to be Pirates

⁓

Mind if I drop anchor?"

It was the kind of question that doesn't wait for an answer. Before I knew it, he was parked on the bar stool next to me, ordering a beer, and a shot of rum. I was nursing a gin and tonic.

"Captain William MacDougall," he said, extending his hand. "But me friends call me Cap'n Billy."

I shook his hand, but mostly I stared. Cap'n Billy was a pirate. His dark hair was long and greasy, as was his beard. His skin was bronze and leathery from too much sun. He wore the skull and crossbones on his head, and a gold ring in his ear. He smelled salty and musty and a bit fishy. And he had the pirate accent down pat.

"Nice to meet you, Cap'n Billy," I said. "Do you work

at a theme park?" I regretted the question as soon as it left my mouth.

"Arrrrgh! A theme park?!" he snapped. "I work on me ship, you scurvy dog! Haven't you ever met a REAL pirate before?"

He paused for a moment and said, with a wink, "I'll forgive ye if you'll buy me a drink."

I motioned to the bartender to bring him another round. Cap'n Billy told the bartender to leave the bottle and put it on my tab.

There was naturalness about the captain that made me feel he wasn't putting on an act. I had never met a real pirate before, but then, where would I have? I live in the suburbs in Ohio—the only coast I'm near is the coast of Kentucky. Cap'n Billy didn't look like the type you'd run into at Starbucks. It was only by chance that I had stopped for a drink at the Crow's Nest Tavern while vacationing near the ocean.

"So you're saying you're a REAL pirate?" I asked.

"Do whales fart in the ocean?" he said. "Of course I'm a real pirate!"

Cap'n Billy took a long draw on the bottle and wiped his mouth on his sleeve. When he raised the bottle to his lips, I noticed a long scar along his forearm.

"Wow, how'd you get that?" I asked.

"Knife wound," he said. "My nickname's 'The Butcher'—'Billy the Butcher.'"

I swallowed the lime in my gin and tonic as I looked frantically for the nearest door, just in case I needed to make a quick exit. I didn't want to have to call my wife from the hospital to explain how I got in a knife fight with a pirate.

"The Butcher?" I asked. "H-H-H-How many men did you have to kill to get that name?"

"I didn't kill anyone," he said with a laugh. "I worked in me dad's butcher shop as a boy and the name stuck to me like a barrrrrnacle on a bowsprit. One day, I was cutting chops with a cleaver and sliced into me arrrrrrrrrrm." Cap'n Billy always emphasized his Rs.

"So, how exactly does one become a REAL pirate?" I asked.

He leaned back and looked off into the distance. I could tell it was going to be a long story but worth the price of the drinks I was buying him.

"I was born in a long line of shipbuilders," Cap'n Billy began. "Me mother gave birth to me outside a pub where the crew from a local shipyard was waiting to get in. From that moment, the sea was in me blood."

Cap'n Billy told me how his mother wrapped him in a sail instead of a blanket. He teethed on hardtack and could pilot a ship by the time he was eight. In grade school a speech therapist tried to help him stop rolling his Rs, to no avail. (Cap'n Billy called her a "speech therrrrapist.")

"When I was 12, I set sail with Captain Robert 'Rat-castle' Rackham," he said. "I was his cabin boy, and he taught me the pirate ways as we sailed the Caribbean." I was beginning to think Cap'n Billy was for real.

"How did you meet Captain Rackham?" I asked.

"My elementary school had a job shadowing program," he said. "I signed up to spend a day learning about life at sea and didn't make it home for five years. By that time, I was Cap'n Rackham's chief gunner. Rackham had a soft spot for me. When he died, he left me his ship, *The Frightened Flounder*."

"How'd he die?" I asked.

"Blew up," Cap'n Billy said. "He got the idea to get rid of his bilge rats using gunpowder. It got rid of the rats alright. It also got rid of the bottom of his ship and him with it. Took me six months to repair the hole in the hull."

At 18, Cap'n Billy had been the youngest pirate captain ever. Over the next 30 years, he visited four continents, 412 ports and 10,242 bars. (There may have been a fifth continent in there somewhere, but he couldn't remember.) He gained a reputation as one of the wisest pirates and was often asked to settle disputes between his peers. And, no matter what port he was in, he never had trouble putting together a crew. Every pirate wanted to sail with "Billy the Butcher."

After an hour, he began to get bored telling the stories he'd told hundreds of times before. "So, what do you do?" he asked.

"I'm a writer," I said.

Cap'n Billy's eyes bulged as he grabbed my arm. "You write?!" he gasped, pressing his face so close to mine I could see pieces of crab cake from lunch—or maybe breakfast—still stuck between his teeth. He seemed like the type who would eat crab cakes for breakfast.

"Take out yer notebook," he ordered.

When I told him I didn't have a notebook, he threw a pile of cocktail napkins in front of me. "Grab a pen. You're going to write down everything I say."

"What am I writing—your biography?" I asked.

Raising children as pirates is like dusting your living room with a leaf blower

If you ask a father, "Would ye like to raise yer wee children as pirates?" you'll get an immediate, enthusiastic "Aye aye!" Ask a mother the same question and you'll get a puzzled, questioning glare.

The reason for the difference is genetic. A person's gender is determined by the presence—or absence—of the Y chromosome. Men have the Y chromosome; women do not. Without going into a text-book lecture about genetics, all you need to know is that the "Y" in "Y chromosome" is short for, "<u>Why</u> don't we raise our kids as pirates, honey?" Men don't have to think about the reasons for raising children as pirates because they intuitively know the great benefits of doing so. It is the same Y chromosome that allows men to intuitively know the answer to, "Why don't I try to dust the inside of the house using a leaf blower?"

In all likelihood, most men have already skipped ahead to the section about converting the family minivan into a pirate schooner and are in the garage beginning the project. Converting a minivan into a pirate schooner is such a compelling project for men that they

would do it even if it meant they had to raise their children as rodeo clowns. (Legal disclaimer: Raising your children as rodeo clowns is an extremely bad idea, unless you want your children to grow into adults who wear heavy makeup, taunt other people, and then hide in barrels.)

Women have an X chromosome instead of a Y chromosome. Studies show that the primary purpose of the X chromosome is to cross out–and negate–ideas created by beings that possess the Y chromosome. Men's personal experiences will bear this out.

Because the Y chromosome creates ideas that are difficult for women to comprehend, it isn't immediately apparent to women why they'd want to raise their children as pirates. In fact, when men raise the topic, women usually respond with one of two statements. Either:

"That's the stupidest thing I've ever heard."

or

"Next to the time you thought it was a good idea to use the leaf blower to dust the living room, that's the stupidest thing I've ever heard."

But in a recent survey of women who had attempted to raise their children as pirates, 97 percent said they loved the idea once they tried it. One hundred percent of those surveyed still said dusting the house with a leaf blower was a stupid idea.

"What good would that do?" he snarled. "I'm going to tell you how to raise kids to be pirates, and you're going to put it all in a book."

It had never occurred to me to raise my kids as pirates. The idea was immediately appealing. I'd read dozens of parenting books, and most of them were full of nonsense like, "treat your children as equals," or "never raise your voice to your children." Raising your kids as pirates didn't seem nearly as crazy as those ideas.

"Do you have any kids?" I asked.

"What's that got to do with it?" he sneered.

"I thought maybe it would be good if you had some expertise in the subject."

"You think having kids makes you a parenting expert?" he laughed. "That's like saying Cap'n Rackham was an extermination expert because he blew up some rats. I've been at sea for six months with a crew of 40 and not only made it through, I enjoyed every minute of it. You spend a few hours in your minivan with your kids and can't handle it."

I couldn't argue. Our drive to the shore to begin our vacation had been miserable and I'd had no control over our four kids.

"Besides," he said. "We've got satellite TV and Internet on *The Frightened Flounder*. I watch *Dr. Phil* every chance I get and have read every 'Dear Abby' column for the past 15 years."

Cap'n Billy was a self-professed parenting guru. A rum-swilling, ship-sailing, treasure-plundering, skull-and-crossbones-wearing, self-professed parenting guru.

"But why do you want kids to be raised as pirates?" I asked.

Cap'n Billy explained that there was a real shortage of pirates—no one to carry on the pirate arts and traditions. Some of the best people he'd ever known had been pirates. The solution was obvious to him—get parents to teach their kids to be pirates. According to the captain, the trouble was today's parents didn't know the benefits of raising their kids as pirates—and they certainly didn't know how to go about doing it.

While I was intrigued by the concept of raising my kids as pirates, I wasn't convinced my wife would be as receptive.

"If ye raised yer little powder monkeys as pirates, you'd be as happy as a bilge rat in a bunghole!" he said.

I had an idea what a bilge rat was but no idea what

a bunghole was or why a rat would be happy in one. It was only much later that Cap'n Billy explained that a bunghole is the spot where the tap goes into a keg of rum or ale.

"There be many good reasons to raise your children as pirates, me hearty," continued the captain. "Your kids may already act as rotten as pirates. If they were pirates, it would help you explain their behavior to other people. Say, you're in the grocery store and your children are destroying the produce section. All you need to say to the manager is, 'Arrgh! Me kids have been at sea for months and are looking for oranges to prevent the scurvy.' The produce manager will be apologizing to you, matey."

"That seems a little far fetched," I said.

"Perhaps," he admitted. "You want your children to have high self-esteem, don't ye? Pirates have the highest self-esteem of any occupation, except the occupation of 'actor.' But you don't want your children to be chased by paparazzi everywhere they go. Pirates are never chased by paparazzi...unless the pirate is Johnny Depp at the opening of *Pirates of the Caribbean*...but that doesn't count because he's not a real pirate."

"High self-esteem is important," I agreed.

"Raising your children as pirates will teach them discipline, hard work, and a colorful vocabulary. Typical household chores become exciting—and fun—when done in the pirate way. Your children may not want to sweep the kitchen floor but they'll beg for the chance to 'swab the poop deck,' even if it's only because they can say the word 'poop' without being flogged for it."

Getting my kids to do chores did sound great. Cap'n Billy could tell I was interested.

"And young pirates are much more likely to listen to their parents," he continued. "Your son may not obey you when you say, 'Stop fighting with your sister,' but he'll listen when you bellow, 'Avast ye scurvy dog or I'll give ye a taste of me hook!'"

Wow, kids who obey—that sounded like a miracle!

"But the best part," said Cap'n Billy, "is that pirates are happy, deal well with difficult circumstances, and are team players. They be financially independent and rarely live with their parents past age 18. And they love their mothers, as is often indicated by their tattoos. What more could you want for your little urchins?"

I was sold. I wanted my kids to be all those things. But I wondered if my kids WANTED to be pirates.

"I know what ye be thinking," Cap'n Billy said. "I've never met a lad or lassie who disliked the idea of being raised as a pirate. Boys are particularly enamored with the 'optional bathing' part of piracy as well as the expanded vocabulary. Girls seem more taken with the constant singing and ability to wear whatever they want. Pirate children are happy—and so be their pirate parents."

Cap'n Billy explained the problem was that parents had no idea how to teach their little landlubbers how to plunder, hornswaggle, and quell mutinies so they could become self-respecting swashbucklers of the high seas or suburbs.

"You probably don't know a gunnel from a galleon," said the captain. "But don't ye fret—Billy 'the Butcher' is here to help."

Cap'n Billy promised to tell me everything he knew about pirate parenting if I'd put it all in a book—everything from how to feed a young pirate ("keep lots of salt cod on hand") to developmental issues, such as when most pirates begin to talk (according to the captain, usually "just before they're about to walk the plank").

"After you finish the book, parents everywhere will

be able to raise their little power monkeys as pirates," said the captain. "They'll be happy, healthy kiddies who have high self-esteem as well as the skills to commit high treason. But most importantly, there'll be more pirates. Lots more pirates."

I spread out a cocktail napkin and clicked open my pen. For the next seven hours, Cap'n Billy told me everything I needed to know to raise my children as pirates. He answered every question I threw at him. His advice filled 119 napkins—both sides.

I followed Cap'n Billy's advice and today, all four of my kids are pirates—happy, energetic pirates who would make any parent proud. And, as promised, I wrote down the captain's words of wisdom, so you can raise your kids as pirates, too. I even polled parents to get their most perplexing pirate parenting questions and had Cap'n Billy answer them.

So, what are ye waiting for, me bucko, a cannon ball through yer mizzen mast? Be a pirate parent. Your children will thank ye for it. And your entire family will be as happy as a bilge rat in a bunghole.

Cap'n Billy's top 10 reasons to raise your children as pirates:

(10)

Give a man a fish, and you feed him for a day. Teach him to be pirate, and he'll steal other people's fish for a lifetime.

(9)

Divvying up booty is good quality time with the kids.

(8)

When other parents hear you're raising your children as pirates, they'll stop asking you to volunteer at school.

(7)

It's fun to watch the emergency room doctor's reaction when you say your son was injured during "a little mishap boarding a merchant vessel that refused to surrender."

(6)

You've always preferred the title "Captain" to "Mommy" or "Daddy."

(5)

You can spend your kids' college savings on more important things, like a trip to Las Vegas.

(4)

Your children already smell like pirates, so the transition will be easy.

(3)

The family that plunders together, stays together!

(2)

Replacing "family movie night" with "family terrorizing the neighbors with cannons night" is a wonderful change of pace.

(1)

Cap'n Billy wants you to do it—and the last person who didn't do what Cap'n Billy asked was set adrift in a rowboat with only a day's supply of water.

PART II:

Captain Billy "The Butcher" MacDougall's Guide to Pirate Parenting

Baby Pirates—
Mapping Out Your Child's Future

⌒

So you're expecting a baby or maybe already have one. Congratulations! Cherish every moment because it will seem like the blink of an eye before your baby turns 18 years old, sets sail, and you get a letter from a foreign port asking for bail money. (That's if you're smart enough to follow the advice in this book.)

You may be nervous about the prospect of taking care of a baby and clueless about the special needs of an infant pirate. Not to fear, Cap'n Billy is here!

Common questions from parents

My wife and I are expecting our first baby pirate. How can we gain confidence regarding how to take care of him?

Many parents are nervous about the birth of their

first child. Cap'n Billy recommends a unique training technique to learn about baby care. Visit your local fish market and purchase a fresh, whole squid and take care of it *as if it were a real baby*. This accomplishes two goals:

1. It gives you practice dressing a baby and changing its diaper.
2. It provides many embarrassing situations similar to those you will experience with your real child.

The average squid wears a size 2T baby outfit. Dress your squid, put it in a stroller and take it for a walk. If someone asks if he or she can see your baby, explain that your baby looks like a squid because, after all, it IS a squid. If the person asks you why you are walking a squid—lie. It is a very bad idea to say, "A pirate named Cap'n Billy 'The Butcher' MacDougall told me walking a fresh, whole squid would help me be a better parent." Most people do not have the good sense to read this book and won't be able to appreciate Cap'n Billy's wisdom. Instead, tell the person that you saw a show on *The Food Network* that recommended marinating squid in fresh air as a natural way to tenderize it. Before long, all of your neighbors will be walking their fish, meat, and poultry in a stroller.

One warning: There are some differences between real babies and squid. Perhaps the most important difference is what comes out of a squid (i.e., ink) is edible. Really. Squid ink is used as a food coloring and flavoring. But what comes out of a real baby (i.e., not squid ink) is not edible. Do not confuse the two, or at least not when you've invited the in-laws over for dinner.

Can I substitute a live monkey for the squid?

If you have access to a live monkey, by all means use it to learn how to take care of a baby! Many pirates keep monkeys as pets, so it's also the perfect playmate for your new baby, once he or she is born. But don't be disappointed when you realize the monkey is cleaner and more polite your child.

My grandmother's name is Elsie and she wants us to name our new pirate after her. But I don't think Elsie is a good pirate name. Am I right?

A good pirate name depends on the pirate's reputation and nickname more than his or her proper name. While Elsie sounds like a better name for a cow than a pirate, it can easily be transformed into Elsie "Cannon

Fire" Johnson or "Smelly Breath" Elsie Johnson, both of which are fine pirate names. This technique can even give peaceful people, such as the Amish, top-of-the-line pirate names. Who wouldn't be terrified of Samuel 'The Plower' Beiler or Rebecca 'Bloody Quilt' Fisher?

I've never changed a baby's diaper before. How do I "swab the poop deck?"

Changing a baby's diaper is no different than swabbing a ship's deck, assuming the deck is covered with a horrendous quantity of pasty, mustard-colored poop. If your ship's deck isn't covered with poop, then changing a diaper is nothing like swabbing a deck. It's more like trying to clean mud off a squealing, squirmy piglet while a skunk crawls up your nose. Cap'n Billy's tip for cleaning mud off a pig while inhaling a skunk is to do it as quickly as possible.

What's the best way to potty train my pirate?

Fill your toilet with small toy ships and let your pirate fire away. Reward your child with chocolate doubloon gold coins for direct hits. Remind your child to activate "the giant whirlpool that brings all vessels to Davy Jones's locker" when he's finished.

When do most pirates begin to talk?

Most pirates will talk (and give you the answers you want) just before they're about to walk the plank.

No, I mean at what age do BABY pirates begin to talk?

Baby pirates don't usually do anything that warrants making them walk the plank. In fact, baby pirates often haven't learned to walk at all. But baby pirates begin to make sounds such as "goo" and "gaa" at about three months. By 18 months, they're usually able to say simple things, such as, "I want me bottle, ye scurvy dog," and "When do we set sail?"

My pirate often says, "The cat has kittened in me mouth." What does she mean by that?

For older pirates, the phrase refers to the taste in one's mouth after a hard night of drinking. But because your baby pirate doesn't drink yet, it may mean she has actually been putting your cat in her mouth. Most young pirates outgrow this habit by age three.

Our one-year-old pirate bangs on everything — silverware on the table, toys on furniture, etc. What should we do about his behavior?

While banging on everything is not normal behavior, it can be useful to have a few bangers in every crew. Give your son a knife and a hammer and put him in front when you're boarding other ships. He's likely to do well in hand-to-hand combat.

I need to pick a pediatrician for my pirate. What questions should I ask potential doctors?

Cap'n Billy suggests these questions to help find a good pirate doctor:

• *Do you have any formal medical training, or did you learn medicine by apprenticing with another ship's doctor?*

• *Do we always have to come to your office, or could I call you on the telephone so you can tell me how to remove my son's hook from our next-door neighbor?*

• *Since you know how to suture, can we bring our sails to you when they need mending?*

• *May we bring our parrot to you when it is sick?*

• *Is there a separate co-pay for the parrot?*

- *In your waiting room, do you have* Celebrity Pirate Magazine*?*
- *In lieu of payment for treatment, will you accept a percentage of my pirate's future pillaging?*

My little pirate seems to be developing slower than many of my friends' pirates. What's normal development for a pirate?

Few pirates are "normal." While there are milestones your pirate should reach by certain ages, they are only guidelines. Some pirates lag a little behind others. And, as Cap'n Billy knows, lagging behind can leave you sitting on the dock watching your ship and its crew sail away without you. In Cap'n Billy's case, the problem wasn't developmental it was "development-ale." He had been drinking and couldn't find his ship before it left port. But most pirates can do the following tasks by the age indicated below.

Hand-eye coordination

One year: Picks up a handful of gunpowder.

Three years: Fills a small cannon with gunpowder.

Five years: Hits a merchant vessel with a cannon ball from 400 yards away.

Walking

One year: Can "cruise" along furniture by walking while holding onto the edge of a chair or couch.

Three years: Able to walk to the television to change the channel whenever Tom Cruise is on.

Five years: Cruises the ocean while navigating a 20-foot ship in a 30-knot wind.

Drinking

One year: Can drink from a sippy cup.

Three years: Can drink from an open cup.

Five years: Can remove a bottle cap by taking out his glass eye and using his eye socket as an opener.

Sleeping

One year: Sleeps eight hours during the night and takes two naps during the day.

Three years: Sleeps eight hours per night without any naps during the day.

Five years: Sleeps while on watch, as long as the captain isn't around.

Separation

One year: Waves "bye-bye."

Three years: Says "bye-bye."

Five years: Puts a note in a bottle and tosses it in the ocean.

Drawing

One year: Holds a crayon and scribbles.

Three years: Draws simple pictures with a crayon.

Five years: Draws a treasure map and threatens to "introduce you to 'Johnny Corkscrew' if you look at it."

Teething

One year: Gets first tooth.

Three years: Loses first tooth.

Five years: Gets first gold tooth.

Our pirate is trying to walk but never crawled. Should I be concerned?

Some doctors believe walking before crawling creates problems that surface later in life. Cap'n Billy agrees. Pirates who walked before crawling have difficulty with pub crawls. Pub Crawls (also called "rum crawls") involve walking (and eventually crawling) from one pub to the next over a period of four or five hours (or days). Pirates who can't crawl are left behind to pick up the tab.

We want to pick a good babysitter for our pirate. How should we go about choosing one?

Cap'n Billy says you can't be too careful picking a babysitter or a ship's captain. In many ways the two positions are alike. Both are positions of responsibility. Interviewing potential babysitters will make you feel more comfortable as well as allow you to get to know the sitter. Ask potential babysitters the following questions:

- *What is the largest mutiny you have quelled?*
- *Can you tie any of these knots: Bowline? Hangman's knot? Lobster buoy hitch? Oysterman's stopper knot? More importantly, can you untie these knots if my children tie you up using them?*
- *Do you have any experience putting out galley fires?*
- *Do you have any experience starting galley fires?*
- *If there's a hurricane blowing from the east and your ship is headed into the wind, on which side should you throw out your storm anchor (a) port (b) starboard (c) bow (d) stern or (e) all of the above. (If you answered "(e) all of the above," what*

were you doing with four storm anchors on your ship?)

After carefully evaluating the answers from all potential baby sitters, pick the one with the least experience. Those with high scores are likely to be pirates and pirates are notoriously bad babysitters.

Prepare a sheet with vital information for your sitter, including where you're going, the alias you will be using while out, and what to do if the police call asking for your whereabouts. For emergencies, also include the phone number of your doctor, dentist, accountant, taxidermist, tattoo parlor, and marina owner. Be clear regarding what is expected of the babysitter and whether you plan to ever return.

Are there any good nursery rhymes to read to baby pirates? Most of the traditional ones don't seem appropriate.

Cap'n Billy has rewritten many nursery rhymes so they're appropriate for pirates. Try reading these to your buccaneers.

There Was an Old Pirate

(There Was an Old Woman)

There was an old pirate who lived on a boat,

Had so many children, couldn't keep it afloat!

He fed them some cod he baked into a torte,
And gave them all daggers and sent them to port.

What are Pirate Crews Made of?
(What Are Little Boys Made Of?)

What are pirate crews made of?
Scurvy and hooks and mean, dirty looks,
That's what pirate crews are made of.

What are pirate captains made of?
Orders and rum and really big guns,
That's what pirate captains are made of.

Monday's Pirate (Monday's Child)

Monday's pirate has a scarred face,
Tuesday's pirate is a head case,
Wednesday's pirate is full of rum,
Thursday's pirate smells like chum,
Friday's pirate is good with a sword,
Saturday's pirate has gold to hoard,
And the pirate that's born on the day that's last,
Is dirty and lies and gets tied to the mast.

Cap'n Billy's baby training tips

Some do, some don't

Babies differ. For example, if you ask 100 parents if their babies suck their thumbs, the results will be split. Some babies do, some don't. Pirates differ, too. If you ask 100 pirates if they'd rather be flogged or clubbed, the results will be split. Some will toss you overboard and the others will stick you with a dagger. Every pirate is unique and so is your new baby! Don't worry if your child is slightly off from your friends' babies. Most pirates are slightly off.

Using a pacifier

Babies often find sucking on a pacifier relaxing. Cap'n Billy still uses a pacifier, only his pacifier is a blunderbuss—a shotgun-like pistol he wields to pacify those trying to board his ship without permission. Nothing relaxes the captain more than retarding an enemy invasion. Consider getting a toy blunderbuss for your baby.

Smells like pirates

Deodorize your baby's diaper pail by filling the bottom with raw fish. The raw fish smell will reduce the diaper smell, and the combination of the two will get your baby used to the stench found in the quarters of most pirate ships.

Hi ho, hi ho, it's off to the brig I go

Buy a playpen and put your baby in it for at least three hours each day. It's good practice for the inevitable weeks spent in the brig later in life.

Bath time — here today, gone tomorrow

If you baby doesn't like to take baths, try making bath time fun! Build a small plank that your baby can use to push dolls into the tub. Your baby will laugh with glee as each doll meets its doom. If your pirate is like most, he or she will stop bathing altogether by age ten or eleven.

Hide your weapons

Put all swords, daggers, pistols, cannons, and gunpowder out of reach of your baby. Your pirate will have plenty of time to play with these things when he is four or five.

Your pirate's progress

Cap'n Billy says there are ten traits that show your new baby has great potential to be a pirate. Check off each one that applies to your child.

☐ When mom's water broke, the baby yelled, "I sail with the tide!"

☐ When the doctor slapped your baby's bottom, the baby slapped the doctor back and then grabbed the doctor's head with the forceps.

☐ In the hospital nursery, your baby stole blankets and pacifiers from the other infants and then denied it.

☐ Other babies' ankle bands say "Baby Girl" or "Baby Boy." Your child's says "Baby Pirate."

☐ When the hospital photographer took a picture of your baby, your baby asked if it was for the wanted posters.

☐ You found your baby in the hospital cafeteria telling stories about his most recent voyage.

☐ Your physician asked "Do hooks run in the family?"

☐ Your baby doesn't have any teeth —just like most adult pirates.

☐ During labor, your spouse shouted things you thought only came out of the mouths of pirates.

☐ By the time your baby left the hospital, the doctors and nurses were calling him "Captain."

If you checked six or more items, your baby has fantastic potential to become a pirate and may even be officer material. You're off to a great start!

Belly Timber—
Feeding Your Pirate

~

"Ye can't plunder on an empty stomach," says Cap'n Billy. Feeding your children the right belly timber helps them grow strong and prepares them for a full day of pirating. But, while you want to feed your young pirate well, don't worry too much about what your little buccaneer eats. When you've been at sea for eight weeks, your standards about what constitutes "high-quality food" decrease considerably. Cap'n Billy once survived for an entire week on nothing but seagull droppings. Eventually, he caught one of the seagulls, which made for a tasty treat.

Common questions from parents

My wife and I are vegetarians. Is it acceptable to substitute tofu for meat in a pirate's diet?

Cooks have walked the plank for less. When Cap'n Billy was a cabin boy, he knew a ship's cook who ran out of meat and served tofu to the crew as a substitute. Shortly after the meal, the "Flying Dutchman Wedgie" was invented. The Flying Dutchman differs from the traditional wedgie in two important ways: (1) The recipient is lifted off the ground and spun around in a circle during the wedgie. (2) Before the recipient is lifted off the ground, his underwear is filled with tofu.

At what age should I wean my little pirate from his bottle?

Pirates are never fully weaned from bottles—the liquid in the bottle just changes as they get older.

I have a six-month-old pirate and want to introduce solid food as soon as possible. What do you recommend?

There are many baby food flavors that provide good variety while mimicking a typical pirate's diet at sea. Here are some menu suggestions:

- Pureed Salt Cod
- Salt Cod and Rice (heavy on the salt cod)
- Rice and Salt Cod (light on the rice)

- Salt Cod Medley (salt cod combined with chunks of salt cod)
- Salt Cod and Salt Cod with Salt Cod in a Salt Cod sauce
- Cheerios

Cheerios help infants learn to pick up small objects and improve hand-eye coordination, which is useful to help fix sails and sew up wounds in crew mates.

What exactly is salt cod?

Cod is a large bottom-dwelling fish found in northern Atlantic waters. Salt cod is a cured food, similar to smoked salmon. It tastes just like chicken, assuming the chicken you're eating spent three months in the belly of a fish and was then buried in salt for a week.

What is the best way to cook salt cod?

Rinse the fish and cut it into pieces. Place the pieces in a dish of cold water and soak in the refrigerator for 24 hours. Change the water several times during the day. Prior to dinner, drain the fish and place it in the trash can. Order pizza.

I want to expose my pirate to different foods, but he shows no interest and insists on eating the same things day after day. What can I do?

Cap'n Billy says you have nothing to worry about. Eating the same food day after day is great practice for being at sea. Pirates often subsist for months on hardtack—a biscuit made with only flour and water. Limiting your little pirate's food choices also cuts down on the amount of time you need to spend in the kitchen. Many parents find they're too busy to make homemade hardtack. Try purchasing a dozen biscuits at a fast food restaurant and leave them in the backseat of your car for a week or two. The result is a substance very similar to hardtack. If you live up north, a hockey puck can provide a suitable substitute for hardtack, although the puck may have more flavor and be easier to chew.

I'm worried about my child's school lunch program. It seems the principal doesn't appreciate it when my pirate steals his classmates' lunches. What should I do?

Plundering sandwiches and other lunch items is a first step toward plundering merchant vessels. Reward your son for his initiative but warn him about the perils of getting caught. He should bribe the principal with half of the food he "acquires." It might also help for him to remind those he is plundering that "dead men tell no tales about missing Twinkies."

My first-grader keeps asking me to stop packing "jet-sam" in his lunch. What does he mean?

Flotsam is an item that has accidentally fallen overboard and is floating in the ocean. Jetsam is an item that was thrown overboard on purpose, for example to make a ship lighter in rough weather. When it comes to lunches, whether a food item is flotsam or jetsam depends on intent. A chocolate chip cookie found on the floor is almost always flotsam, because no child in his right mind would throw it away. On the other hand, the carrot sticks you pack in your pirate's lunch are top-of-the-line jetsam. Another term young pirates use for throwing away food they dislike is, "keelhauling the food pyramid."

Do you have any recipes for cute pirate birthday cakes with little ships on top?

No, you have this book confused with the book, *Martha Stewart Parenting*.

What is scurvy and how can I change my pirate's diet to prevent it?

Scurvy is a sickness that makes a person look pale, with liver spots on the skin. It is caused by a deficiency of Vitamin C. Often, because pirates spend weeks at sea, they do not eat enough foods that contain Vitamin C. Cap'n Billy always puts a slice of lemon in his rum to help prevent scurvy. He's been know to take that medication 10-12 times per day, just to be safe. Advanced cases of scurvy have been known to cause death. Advanced cases of Cap'n Billy's medicinal rum have caused him to be dead drunk.

My skin is pale and I have liver spots. Do I have scurvy?

You may have scurvy or you may be Elizabeth Taylor. If you've been married more than 30 times, you're most likely Elizabeth Taylor. If you haven't been married that often, check with your doctor to get a medical opinion.

Besides Vitamin C to prevent scurvy, are there other vitamins I should give my pirate?

Vitamin R is important for pirate health. Vitamin R can be found in sulfurrrrrh, copperrrrrh and phosphorrrrrrhus. You know you're child is getting enough Vitamin R by asking him or her to repeat this sentence: "I parked my car at Harvard Yard." If it sounds like, "I parrrrrrked my carrrrrrh at Harrrrrrvard Yarrrrrrrd," your child is getting plenty of Vitamin R.

I've noticed that you don't see many fat pirates. Is there something about the pirate diet and lifestyle that keeps them thin?

According to Cap'n Billy, there are three things that contribute to pirates being thin: Bad food, not enough food, and the fact that fat pirates are the first jetsam during stormy weather.

Has Cap'n Billy written any nursery rhymes about pirate food?

Yes he has! Your little pirates will love these:

First Mate Larry (Mary, Mary, Quite Contrary)

First mate Larry, big and hairy,
How does your belly grow?
With salted cod and pickled scrod,
And spicy squid-baked dough.

Cutthroat Joe (Jack and Jill)

Cutthroat Joe went down below,
To fetch a piece of hardtack,
Joe fell down and almost drown'd,
The hold was filled with water.

Up swam Joe and bail'd the hole,
As fast as he could manage,
Patched the hull with pris'ners' skulls,
And then went back to dinner.

Bloody Jack Fredrick (Little Jack Horner)

Bloody Jack Fredrick sat on the poop deck,
Eating a bilge rat pie.
He took a great bite, then said with delight,
"Tis moldy I can't deny!"

Cap'n Billy's diet and nutrition tips

Pirate food groups

Keep the two preferred pirate food groups in mind whenever you're planning a meal. The two pirate food groups are:

1. Meat (preferably of an animal)

2. Rum (preferably in a large container)

Because young pirates aren't legal drinking age, parents have to drink their children's rum for them. That's one of the bonuses of pirate parenting.

Rock the boat

Pirates are messy eaters, not because they're sloppy, but because they usually eat at a table that rocks with the waves. To mimic this effect, attach the rockers from a rocking chair to the legs of your kitchen table. This trains children to eat during a Category Five hurricane. It also cuts down on dinner time activities such as food throwing because it is difficult to get you hands on the food when it's sliding around the table.

Plenty of roughage

Fiber is important to your child's diet and is surprisingly easy to find aboard ship—as long as you're willing to eat rope. Prepare rope dishes for your child so he or she will get used to the unique taste. (Make sure to use manila or hemp rope and NOT rope made from nylon or polypropylene.) Two of Cap'n Billy's favorite rope dishes are Rope Shiraz with Porcini and Whole Shallots, and Rope with Roasted Lemons, Green Olives, and Capers.

Your pirate's progress

According to Cap'n Billy, there are ten things overheard at the dinner table that show your child is quickly becoming a pirate. Check each one that your child has said in the past three months.

❏ "You can flog me but I'm not eating creamed spinach."

❏ "I've buried me treasure in the mashed potatoes."

❏ "I'll need another ration of grog if you expect me to eat these peas."

❏ "Your tuna noodle casserole would be perfect to fill cracks in the deck."

❏ "This chicken tastes like the parrot I was forced to eat after being marooned on an island for 30 days."

❏ "I wouldn't serve brussel sprouts even to the prisoners in the brig."

❏ "If I eat all my food, can I plunder the neighbors before I go to bed?"

❏ "This burger is fatty enough to grease a mast."

❏ "Too many vegetables — too little shark."

❏ "What did they do with the last cook's body after he was hung from the yardarm?"

If you checked six or more items, your child is well on his or her way to becoming a pirate! Give yourself a pat on the back—but not with your arm that has a hook at the end.

Sleeping Like a Sea Dog and Other Nocturnal Issues

⌒

Pirate days are filled with fun—but tiring—activities. A good night's rest is essential, especially for young pirates. But for pirates, there's more than sleep going on during the night. Between nighttime raids, late-night watches, and closing pubs, pirates are busy, busy, busy after dark!

Common questions from parents

Our pirate often wakes in the middle of the night and won't go back to sleep. Is this a serious problem?

Cap'n Billy had that very problem when he was young. The ship's doctor (who was also the ship's cook) diagnosed it as "watch confusion." Cap'n Billy kept waking in the middle of the night because he thought it was his watch. Ship watches are difficult to keep straight. First watch goes from 8 p.m. to midnight. Middle watch is from midnight to 4 a.m. Morning watch goes from 4 a.m. to 8 a.m. Forenoon watch is from 8 a.m. to noon. Afternoon watch is from noon to 4 p.m. First dog watch goes from 4 p.m. to 6 p.m. and last dog watch is from 6 p.m. to 8 p.m., which brings you back to first watch. With so many watches, it's impossible to keep them straight. But by giving the watches names that are meaningful to your pirate, he will be better able to remember them and less likely to wake in the night.

Children never forget the time of television programs, so try renaming the watches based on your child's favorites. This works especially well if your child watches 15-20 hours of television per day, which is the national average. For example, you could rename the ship watches as follows:

Original name/time	New name
First watch	
(8 p.m. to midnight)	*CSI* watch
Middle watch	
(midnight to 4 a.m.)	*Late Show with David Letterman* watch

Morning watch

(4 a.m. to 8 a.m.)   *SpongeBob*

                                  SquarePants watch

Forenoon watch

(8 a.m. to noon)   *Oprah* watch

Afternoon watch

(Noon to 4 p.m.)   *All My Children* watch

First dog watch

(4 p.m. to 6 p.m.)   Evening News watch

Last dog watch

(6 p.m. to 8 p.m.)   *Wheel of Fortune* watch

Be clear as to which watch your child has and your child should stop waking in the middle of the night. Also, make sure to update your watch names with each new television season.

What is a nightmare and how can I prevent them?

Cap'n Billy says a nightmare is when you're being attacked by another ship and you realize that all your gunpowder is wet and unusable. The best way to prevent nightmares is by keeping your gunpowder sealed in dry, airtight containers.

My pirate is eight and still wets his bed. Is there a cure for this?

"Nocturnal enuresis" is the medical term for bed-wetting but Cap'n Billy calls it "Sogging the Quartermaster." Pirates sleep in hammocks strung as many as four on top of each other. If you sleep under a bed wetter, as Cap'n Billy's quartermaster did, you'll run into "foul weather." That's why bed-wetting pirates should always take the bottom hammock. To cure bed-wetting, try these treatments:

- Limit grog rations near bedtime.

- Develop a reward system to encourage your child, such as giving him a three-day shore pass for every dry night.

- Use a bed-wetting alarm so your child wakes whenever he begins to wet the bed. Some of these systems use a buzzer or bell to wake the child whenever wetness is detected. Replace the buzzer or bell with a medium-size cannon. This will teach your child to wake before "Sogging the Quartermaster" occurs. Remember not to put shot in the cannon—just gunpowder. If you add shot, your neighbors will also wake up as a cannon ball goes through their roof.

My pirate has dreams that she's flying. Is this normal?

Strange dreams are normal for pirates. Cap'n Billy has a recurring dream in which he is Marilyn Monroe singing "Happy Birthday" to President John F. Kennedy. Reassure your daughter that it is only a dream. In a waking state, pirates cannot fly, although many have tried unsuccessfully after falling off the rigging. A few pirates have even been "hoisted by their petards," which is a similar to flying. A petard, is a small barrel of gunpowder. If you accidentally set it off, you will fly— albeit briefly and with a rough landing. If your daughter stops eating salt cod right before bed, her flying dreams may go away.

My pirate walks in his sleep. Should I try to wake him?

Sleepwalking or somnambulism, is common among children. It is often difficult to wake a sleepwalker and the sleepwalker may have amnesia when he awakes. Some sleepwalkers have been known to accomplish complex tasks while in a state of slumber. Cap'n Billy heard about a cabin boy who, while sleepwalking, led a mutiny aboard his ship. When the cabin boy awoke, he was the new captain, much to his surprise. So, Cap'n

Billy recommends leaving your sleepwalking pirate alone if he is doing a useful activity, such as rebuilding a ship, interrogating prisoners, or telling you where his treasure is located.

Getting my pirate to go to bed is always a battle. How can I win?

Fighting a bedtime battle is no different than fighting a battle at sea. First tell your child to surrender or "prepare to be boarded." If he resists, take out a wooden paddle and "board his bottom" until he's willing to go to bed.

Has Cap'n Billy written any nursery rhymes to read at bedtime?

Do pirates have wooden legs? Your pirate will love these:

Rock-A-Bye Pirate (Rock-A-Bye Baby)
Rock-a-bye pirate,
in the crow's nest,
Down in the bilge,
the rats they infest.

When the wind howls,

You'll fall from your height,

and land on the captain,

to the crew's delight.

Sleeping Pirate (Georgie Porgie)

Sleeping Pirate, with a glass eye,

Dreamt he was Captain Bligh.

When he woke and sat up straight,

Sad, sad pirate was just first mate.

Hush, Little Pirate (Hush, Little Baby)

Hush, little pirate, don't say a word.

Captain's going to buy you a cutlass sword.

And if that cutlass sword won't slice,

Captain's gonna give you a rope to splice.

And if that rope gets all frayed,

Captain's gonna take you on a pirate raid.

And if that pirate raid is foiled,

Captain's gonna give you cod-liver oil.

And if that cod-liver oil makes you upchuck,
Captain's gonna let the crew run amok.

And when you run, if you fall down,
Don't go overboard or you'll drown.

Cap'n Billy's nighttime training tools

Stumbling in the dark

While your pirate may want a night light in his room, do not allow him to have one. Dependence on artificial light hurts a pirate's night vision. Allow your child to stumble over toys and stuffed animals on the way to the bathroom. It's excellent training for stumbling across deck at 4 a.m. to take a turn at the watch.

Waterbed training

Waterbeds help young pirates get their sea legs long before they ever set sail on the ocean. They provide good practice for sleeping on board a ship and are also good for practicing other pirate tasks. Jump up and down on one end of the bed while your child attempts to do his homework on the other end. This is similar to filling out the captain's logbook in heavy seas. Also have your child try hand-to-hand combat, barrel rolling, and pouring rum, while on the waterbed. *Note:* If your child has already had his hook installed, make sure a plastic hook guard is in place before doing any waterbed activities.

Versatile, dangerous blankies

Your child may become attached to sleeping with a blanket. Once onboard ship, he will be teased for this. There are several solutions that allow your child to keep the blanket while avoiding being teased.

• Draw a skull and crossbones on the blanket and instruct your child to tell others he is "protecting the Jolly Roger" from being stolen during the night.

• Wrap the blanket around your child's head like a pirate head scarf.

• Tell your child to sleep with a sword underneath the blanket. Those who tease him will only tease him once.

Your pirate's progress

Cap'n Billy says there are ten favorite bedtime stories for young pirates. Please check off each story that your child has requested in the last three months.

☐ *Goldilocks and the Three Scurvy Dogs*

☐ *Green Eggs and Hardtack*

☐ *Chicka Chicka Boom Boom Goes the Cannon During Battle*

☐ *Harry Potter and the Giant Squid That Ripped Him Limb from Limb*

☐ *One Beard, Two Beards, Red Beard, Blue Beard*

☐ *Oh, the Places You'll Go After You Get Off This Infernal Deserted Island"*

☐ *The Runaway Bunny is Eaten by the Ravenous Crew*

☐ *The Cat in the Hat Walks the Plank*

☐ *Beauty and the Beastly Cap'n Billy*

☐ *Snow White and the Seven Ports*

If you checked five or more items, your child has great taste in literature and is also a buccaneer in the making! To celebrate your child's progress, have the entire family watch Pirates of the Caribbean *tonight. If you don't own the movie, find a neighbor who owns it, wait until they're gone for the evening and watch the movie at their house.*

Quelling Mutinies—
Disciplining Your Pirate

Very young children are known for their temper tantrums and outbursts. One day there was an incredible commotion coming from a grocery store. The sound of screaming, kicking, shouting, and boxes tumbling to the floor could be heard blocks away. But that's what happens when Cap'n Billy is in the mood for bean dip and the store is out of his favorite brand.

The most successful pirates are self-centered, self-absorbed, self-assured, self-appointed, self-asserting, self-complacent, self-directed leaders who use self-addressed, self-adhesive envelopes and cook self-basting turkeys in self-cleaning ovens. Unfortunately, many pirates lack self-discipline. Discipline and proper behavior can, however, be taught.

Common questions from parents

Should I use corporal punishment on my pirate?

Cap'n Billy believes in corporal punishment. He also believes in punishing any other officers captured on the merchant vessels he acquires.

No, by "corporal punishment," I mean spanking.

Cap'n Billy has never spanked a corporal but he once gave Corporal Edwin Smythe a "time out." Cap'n Billy's rule is, "One month of time out for every year old the person is." Corporal Smythe was 36 years old, so his time out on a deserted island lasted three years.

Is it appropriate to maroon my pirate?

Marooning is the practice of leaving a pirate on an island where there is little to eat. You can maroon your pirate but, since your pirate is so young, do not maroon him on an island. Maroon him in the produce section of a grocery store. He won't find anything to eat there.

I've heard of using reverse psychology to get children to do what you want. What exactly is reverse psychology and how do I use it?

Reverse psychology is telling your pirate one thing, in the hope he will disobey and do the opposite.

Regular psychology: "Please eat your squid and seaweed casserole. It's good for you."

Outcome: Your pirate says he doesn't like the taste of the casserole and won't eat it.

Reverse psychology: "Please do not eat your squid and seaweed casserole because it's too delicious for you and I want it all for myself."

Outcome: You get the squid and seaweed casserole all to yourself because your pirate says he doesn't like the taste of the casserole and won't eat it.

Quadruple reverse psychology: "Please do not eat your squid and seaweed casserole because it's not too delicious for you not to eat and I do not want it all for myself."

Outcome: Neither you nor your pirate understand what you've said.

What is an effective system to reward positive behavior?

Rewarding positive behavior (aka "bribing") is a long-standing pirate tradition. Use a bribe that will appeal to your pirate. Tell your pirate ahead of time about the reward and reap the great benefits. For example:

Bribe: "If you eat your squid and seaweed casserole, I'll take you to the movies."

Outcome: Your child eats the squid and seaweed casserole and you go to the movies. Later you find a full serving of squid and seaweed casserole stuck to the bottom of your kitchen table.

I have to repeat myself four or five times before my pirate will listen. How can I get him to listen and obey the first time I say something?

Cap'n Billy suggests using a booming voice and being as specific as possible when giving an order. If necessary, use a bullhorn when commanding your pirate. For example: "All hands on deck, we're being attacked by cannon fire from the starboard side!!"

Avoid repeating commands but, if a command isn't followed, repeat it once along with the consequence of not following the command. For example: "I repeat: All hands on deck, we're being attacked by cannon fire from the starboard side!! If you don't defend the ship, we'll be sunk, lose our treasure, and probably die a horrible death, which would make me very angry."

If after repeating the command, your pirate still disobeys and the two of you are still alive, send your child to bed without dessert.

My pirate often relieves himself in public places. What should I do?

Peeing in public is normal pirate behavior and usually doesn't create a major problem. But, under no circumstances, put your child in the crow's nest. Cap'n Billy once sailed with a pirate named Peeing Pete who routinely drank a gallon of water and then went straight to the crow's nest to relieve himself, much to the crew's chagrin. The problem was solved when the crew replaced Peeing Pete's water with kerosene. You see, Peeing Pete was also a smoker.

Is sibling rivalry common among young pirates?

Pirates are often jealous of each other. The oldest pirate may think he should be in command based on age. The youngest pirate may feel frustrated that he can't do all the things older pirates are capable of doing, such as pillaging without adult supervision. If sibling rivalry gets out of hand, tie your pirates up, rub them with bacon grease, and put them near an ant colony for a few hours. This will turn their animosity for each other toward you, putting an end to their rivalry.

Are organized sports a good way to teach my pirate discipline?

Absolutely! Almost any organized sport can teach your child the discipline he needs to be a contributing member of the pirate community. Help your pirate focus on the most important parts of the sports in which he participates. By "most important," Cap'n Billy means, "most important penalties or fouls." Cap'n Billy played many sports as a child and won several awards for unique and aggressive penalties, including:

- Roughing the parrot (also know as a "fowl shot")
- Flogging the kicker
- Three-second violation (not moving away from the front of a cannon quickly enough)
- Personal fowl (stealing someone else's parrot)
- Face masking (tearing the eye patch off another player)
- Illegal use of peg leg

- Offensive mast interference
- Hooking

Are "distraction techniques" useful to get your pirate's attention away from inappropriate behaviors?

Redirecting your pirate's behavior can sometimes work, but it depends on how attractive the inappropriate behavior is compared to the distraction. For example, Cap'n Billy once said to his crew: "Look at that cute seagull over there and stop watching where I'm burying me treasure." Unfortunately, the cute seagull couldn't compare with the lure of treasure, so the crew kept watching Cap'n Billy. He eventually persuaded the crew to shut their eyes by threatening to shoot them. "Death threats" are a severe form of distraction that force the person to consider whether they would rather watch where the treasure is being buried or be buried with the treasure.

What does it mean to use "natural consequences" to teach your pirate the results of his actions?

The best example of natural consequences is Cap'n Billy's old cook, Erik "Lefty" Johanson. One day Erik was trying to catch shrimp near shore in the Florida Keys.

Cap'n Billy warned Erik that a huge alligator had been seen in those parts. Erik ignored the captain's advice, had his right arm chewed off, and was dubbed "Lefty." Losing his arm was the "natural consequence" of not listening to Cap'n Billy. Other pirate nicknames that have come from "natural consequences" include: One-eyed John, Peg-leg Sue, Jimmy the Hook, Toothless Kate, Barnacle Brain Bob, and Tentacle Face Fred.

I read that many ships have rules every pirate is required to sign and obey. Does Cap'n Billy have rules for his ship?

Absolutely! Each member of Cap'n Billy's crew must agree to a list of rules that help his ship run smoothly and ensure that each pirate does his job.

Cap'n Billy's Code of Conduct

• Each man has equal title to fresh provisions, strong liquors (at any time seized) and may use them at pleasure.

• If any man deserts the ship, he shall be marooned with one bottle of water, one small pistol, and one copy of the book *1001 Things to Do When You Have a Lot of Time on Your Hands.*

• No discharging weapons below deck (unless the

shark fin soup is undercooked and attacks).

• If any man loses an eye in battle, he shall receive 200 Pieces of Eight. If he loses a limb, 400, If he loses an autographed picture of Johnny Depp, 600. If he "loses his lunch," another lunch will be provided after the battle.

• He that is found guilty of drunkenness in time of battle shall suffer the punishment the majority of the company see fit, up to and including being forced to watch 20 hours of *Telletubbies* reruns.

• These rules apply only while at sea. While in port, anything goes.

Has Cap'n Billy written any nursery rhymes about pirate discipline?

Does *The Frightened Flounder* have a plank? Of course he has! Your pirates will love these:

Ding Dong Jig (Ding Dong Bell)

Ding dong jig,

Whole crew's in the brig.

Who put 'em in?

Cap'n Johnny Flynn.

Who set 'em free?

The parrot Polly.

What a stupid bird was that,

To dis who wears a captain's hat.

But Polly bird won't squawk no more,

Cause Cap'n smacked her with an oar.

Cap'n Billy (Old MacDonald)

Cap'n Billy had a ship, E-I-Yo-Ho-Ho,

And on his ship he had a crew, E-I-Yo-Ho-Ho,

With an "Arrr, Arrr," here, and an "Arrr, Arrr," there,

Here an "Arrr," there an "Arrr," everywhere

   an "Arrr, Arrr,"

Cap'n Billy had a ship, E-I-Yo-Ho-Ho.

Cap'n Billy had a ship, E-I-Yo-Ho-Ho,

And on his ship he had some rum, E-I-Yo-Ho-Ho,

With a swill, swill, here, and a swill, swill, there,

Here a swill, there a swill, everywhere

   an swill, swill,

Cap'n Billy had a ship, E-I-Yo-Ho-Ho.

Cap'n Billy had a ship, E-I-Yo-Ho-Ho,

And on his ship he had a mutiny, E-I-Yo-Ho-Ho,

With a sword fight, here, and a sword fight, there,

Here a stab, there a slash, everywhere
   an stab, slash,
Cap'n Billy had a ship, E-I-Yo-Ho-Ho.

Cap'n Billy found an island, E-I-Yo-Ho-Ho,
On that isle marooned his crew, E-I-Yo-Ho-Ho,
With a "be gone ye scurvy dogs," here, and a "be gone
   ye scurvy dogs," there,
Here a "scurvy," there a "scurvy," everywhere
   an "scurvy, scurvy,"
Cap'n Billy found an island, E-I-Yo-Ho-Ho.

Nasty Blue Beard (Little Boy Blue)
Nasty Blue Beard come swing your sword,
Your ship's been attacked by rivals in hoards,
But where's the pirate who's turn was on watch?
He fell asleep after drinking too much scotch.
Will you wake him? No, not me — I'll just set him
   adrift in thar blue sea.

Yo Ho, Black Beard (Baa, Baa, Black Sheep)
Yo ho, Black Beard have you any gold?
Aye, matie, down in the hold!

Avast ye thief, don't be laying claim,

To any of me treasure or you'll feel my sword.

Note: Cap'n Billy has always thought protecting treasure is more important than rhyming.

Cap'n Billy's tips for disciplining your pirate

Discipline isn't punishment

Remember, there's a difference between discipline and punishment. The role of discipline is to teach your pirate the appropriate way to act. The role of punishment is to get prisoners to tell you where their booty is located.

Keep your rules simple

Long, complicated rules can't be obeyed because they aren't understood. Keep your rules simple, such as, "Touch it and you'll feel the tip of me sword!" There's no need to elaborate on what "it" is because your pirate will know the instant he feels a sharp pain in his side.

Punish quickly

If you must punish your pirate, do it quickly, before your pirate climbs up the rigging and is hard to catch. It's a nuisance to put rigging back up after you've had to cut it down. And, after the third time you've brought your pirate to the emergency room because he "fell off the rigging," a social services staff member will pay a visit to your house. Most social service agencies don't appreciate the benefits of pirate parenting.

Your pirate's progress

Cap'n Billy says there are ten malicious behaviors that are signs of a healthy young pirate. Please check off each behavior that your child has exhibited in the last 12 months.

☐ Stuck sibling's hook in an electrical outlet.

☐ Replaced all the gunpowder with baking power right before a big battle.

☐ Watered down the rum.

☐ Tried the old putting-black-shoe-polish-on-the-inside-of-dad's-eye-patch trick.

☐ Flushed sibling's goldfish during a "burial at sea" but didn't wait until the fish were dead to do it.

☐ Put termites on Cap'n Billy's wooden leg.

☐ On Halloween, replaced the traditional trick-or-treat greeting with, "Your money or your life!"

☐ Threw live sharks in the neighbor's hot tub.

☐ Told teacher his homework was "eaten by a giant barracuda when the family's ship wrecked on a coral reef near the Dry Tortugas."

☐ Plagarrrrrised a homeworrrrrk reporrrrrrt about Gerrrrald Forrrrrrd.

If you checked four or more items, your child is rotten to the core. You should be proud...but watch your back!

Scurvy and Hook Injuries— Pirate Health & Safety

⁓

Cap'n Billy knows eye patches, missing teeth, peg legs, and hooks are all stunning fashion statements but he suggests trying to keep your pirate safe when he's young. There will be plenty of time for your pirate to get his eye poked out or lose his teeth when he's older and foolishly tries to cheat at cards while playing with Carl "The Slasher" Kowalski. Until then, follow Cap'n Billy's advice so your pirate can be as fit as a fiddler crab.

Common questions from parents
Should my pirate be immunized?
Cap'n Billy recommends the typical childhood immunizations as well as these special pirate vaccines:

WRV: Wood rot vaccine. Prevents peg leg deterioration.

RRV: Rust removal vaccine. Keeps hooks shiny and clean.

HFV: Hempen Fever vaccine, also known as The Anti-Hanging Vaccine. It helps build strong neck muscles.

TMV: Trench Mouth vaccine. Trench Mouth is caused by bacteria often found on the wooden plates pirates use to eat. It can lead to bad breath and a foul taste in your mouth, but then so can most pirate food.

IPA: India Pale Ale vaccine. Special sparkling ale vaccine taken orally in 12-ounce doses. It doesn't prevent anything but it's tasty medicine.

How do I treat common pirate cuts?

Rinse the cut and apply pressure with a clean cloth. If after five minutes the bleeding continues, check carefully to see if an arm or leg has been severed or if there is a hole in your pirate's torso that is the size of a parrot. Reattach the limb or plug the hole with any parrot-sized object. Wait two or three days before beginning a personal vendetta against the person who caused the wound. Do not rub salt in the wound, unless the wound is in a prisoner.

What do I do if my pirate has a tooth knocked out?

If it is a baby tooth, a new tooth will replace it. If it is an adult tooth, don't worry about it because most pirates have missing teeth. If it is a gold tooth, see your local jeweler to have it reinstalled.

Should I teach my pirate to swim?

Swimming is a critical safety skill for pirates. A pirate captain won't risk running his ship aground, so he's unlikely to sail close to shore to maroon you. After what he refers to as "a minor communication problem," Cap'n Billy was tossed overboard three miles from shore. (Young Billy was asked by his captain to clean some "ink scum" off the deck. It was a windy day and, instead of "ink scum," Billy heard "drink rum.") Luckily, Billy was a good swimmer and made it to dry land.

Cap'n Billy suggests calling your local YMCA or other pool-equipped establishment and asking the following questions about the swimming lessons they offer:

1) *Do you teach introductory underwater combat with monsters of the deep? (Most pools will not have REAL sea monsters, so an SMS (sea-monster simulator) is acceptable. Another simulation technique is to have your*

child swim when the local overeater's anonymous club is using the pool.

2) Does the pool have both a high and low plank to practice walking off?

3) Are instructees forced to swim fully clothed with hands tied behind their backs?

4) Do instructors fire warning shots over instructees' heads?

5) Do they teach the "dead man's float?" (This is a trick question because everyone Cap'n Billy knows who did the "dead man's float" had never been taught the stroke but did it perfectly after dying and being throw overboard.)

6) Finally, do they disinfect the showers regularly? (Athlete's Foot is a terrible thing to have while at sea.)

My pirate has swimmer's ear. What exactly is it and how is it cured?

Swimmer's ear is an infection of the ear canal. It can be caused by water forced into the ear during falls into a pool or the ocean. (These falls may be accidental or plank-cidental.) Swimmer's ear causes extreme pain. To prevent swimmer's ear, don't walk the plank or fall overboard.

There are other causes of ear pain, not caused by swimmer's ear. If your child feels sudden ear pain, instruct him or her to look to see if he's been struck in the ear by a crewmate, seagull, or cannon-fired projectile.

My child has ADD. Will that keep him from becoming a good pirate?

By "ADD," Cap'n Billy assumes you mean "Admiral Dirkson's Daughter." Kidnapping the Admiral's daughter will make your son one of the most sought-after and infamous pirates ever.

How can I remove chewing gum from my pirate's hair?

While chewing gum in the hair isn't a serious health issue, it is a nuisance. Cap'n Billy says to rub a small amount of mayonnaise or peanut butter in the hair where the gum is. After working it in for awhile, the gum will come out easily. This solution also works for more serious health issues, such as if a giant octopus wraps its tentacles around your face. If this occurs, apply a large amount of mayonnaise or peanut butter to the octopus and work it into the octopus until the beast slides off. If there isn't any mayonnaise or peanut butter on the ship, stick the octopus with a dagger six or seven hundred times, being careful not to get the knife too close to your face.

What is pinkeye and how can I treat it?

Conjunctivitis or pinkeye is the inflammation of the conjunctiva, the white part of the eye. It is caused by bacteria and viruses, and is extremely contagious. Do not let your child share another pirate's glass eye. While swapping glass eyes may seem like harmless fun, it often spreads disease. To treat conjunctivitis, get a prescription antibiotic from your child's doctor or change your child's nickname to "Pinkeye the Pirate."

What should my pirate know about fire safety?

There is only one thing your pirate needs to know: Never fire until the captain gives the order. Firing without orders is punishable by 16 lashes.

Is it safe to perform the Heimlich maneuver on my pirate?

The Heimlich maneuver, named after Captain Ludwig Von Heimlich, is similar to the Flying Dutchman Wedgie except that a live bilge rat is substituted for the tofu. Von Heimlich used this maneuver as a way to punish crew members considering mutiny and as a way to amuse himself during long, boring weeks at sea. The Heimlich maneuver is not safe to perform on a child or any other person because serious injury can result from having a live bilge rat in your shorts.

So what should I do if my pirate is choking?

Children are naturally curious and will often put things in their mouths that don't belong there—coins, buttons, marbles, hamsters, doorknobs, coffeemakers, spare tires, satellite dishes, and other items that can block their airways. If your child is choking, first open his mouth and try to remove the object with your fingers. If you cannot reach the object, give your child three sharp blows to the back. If the item remains lodged in your child's throat, threaten to perform the Heimlich maneuver. Most children are scared of rats and will cough out whatever is stuck in their throats.

How can I keep my pirate safe on Halloween?

Dress your pirate in light-colored clothing that can be easily seen by drivers. Also attach a round bicycle reflector to your pirate's eye patch and put reflective tape on your pirate's sword, hook, and/or peg leg.

My pirate loves his eye patch so much he won't take it off. He's insisted on wearing it for Halloween the past five years, and his friends are starting to tease him. What can I do to encourage him to try other costumes?

Eye patches are like a pirate's security blanket. They feel uncomfortable when separated from them. Instead of looking for costumes without an eye patch, why not try to make other costumes using your son's eye patch? For example, an eye patch placed on his nose will make him look like a bear. Put one on his chin as a beard, and he can be a beatnik. If he has more than one eye patch—and what pirate doesn't—he can wear one on either cheek as mutton chop sideburns and trick-or-treat as Elvis. Wearing an eye patch on both eyes creates a fine Ray Charles costume but makes it difficult to see where you're going. And remember, the most important part of trick-or-treating isn't the costume, it's terrorizing the neighbors.

Has Cap'n Billy written any nursery rhymes about pirate health and safety?

Not only has he written some, his nursery rhymes teach valuable lessons that may save your pirate's life some day. Read these to your little powder monkeys:

Whittle Whittle Pirate (Diddle Diddle Dumpling)

Whittle whittle pirate, Peg Leg Greg,

Sat right down on a powder keg.

One leg's wood and one's of bone,

Couldn't find either when the keg was blown.

Captain Clapton (Humpty Dumpty)

Captain Clapton fought in a brawl,

Captain Clapton got hit with a maul.

All the ship's doctors and all the ship's crew,

Buried the captain and bid him adieu.

Twinkle, Twinkle, Little Scar
(Twinkle, Twinkle, Little Star)

Twinkle, twinkle, little scar,

How I got you was bizarre,

Now I know it isn't fun,

To get shot up with a gun.

Twinkle, twinkle, little scar,

How I got you was bizarre!

When you're cleaning out the barrel,

You look in it at your peril,

Always make sure it's not loaded,

Cause in my face, it exploded.

Twinkle, twinkle, little scar,

How I got you was bizarre!

The Dirty, Scurvy Pirate (The Itsy, Bitsy Spider)

The dirty, scurvy pirate got a case of the gout,

A painful inflammation that often made him shout.

Every day at noon, the puss he drain'd,

Twas the only thing he found that could help him
ease the pain.

Cap'n Billy's health and safety training tips

Cleans and anesthetizes

After sterilizing surgical implements with alcohol, give
the alcohol to the patient to drink. Alcohol is a wonderful
pain killer for the patient. Plus, if other crew members see
you throwing alcohol away, there'd surely be mutiny.

Don't joke about the plague

The Black Death was a plaque that caused hysteria
and death in the 1300s. The disease was carried by
Oriental rat fleas. Because most pirate ships have

rats, pirates have a morbid fear of The Black Death to this day. To allay those fears, never joke about the Black Death. While it may seem funny at the time, do not call the cook's meatloaf "Black Death." Nor is it appropriate to tease crewmates by asking, "Is that an Oriental rat flea on your head?"

Don't "let" it go

While many pirates still practice bloodletting, modern medicine has proven that bloodletting is ineffective. Instead of trying to convince your pirate that bloodletting is a ridiculous treatment, encourage him to practice medicine by "letting the blood" of those on the ships being attacked.

Remove hooks during electrical storms

Many young pirates remember to put down their swords during lightening storms but forget to remove their metal hooks. The can result in a change in nickname from "hook" to "rotisserie spit."

Your pirate's progress

Cap'n Billy says there are ten common types of illnesses and injuries experienced by young pirates. Please check off each that your child has had in the last 12 months.

❏ Bites from insects, pets, Captain Crazy Eddie Hasenpfeffer, or a great white shark.

❏ Falls off bicycles, skateboards, the crow's nest, or overboard.

❏ Poisoning from Ivy, Sumac, moldy salt cod, or bad rum.

❏ Chicken Pox, electric shocks, wet socks, or a ship on the rocks.

❏ Minor cuts and abrasions from tripping on hard surfaces, bumping into things, sword play, or major skirmishes involving hostile parties trying to guard their booty.

❏ Allergic reactions to peanuts, pollen, flogging, or work.

❏ Motion sickness from long car trips, amusement park rides, or sailing a small galleon in a Category Five hurricane.

❏ The flu, an ocean view, loose screws, or a mutinied crew.

❏ Head lice, ring worm, barnacles, or bilge rats.

❏ Projectile vomiting or, as Cap'n Billy likes to call it, "feeding the flounder," "hurling hardtack," "firing the big gun," "visiting Admiral Ralph," "giving it the old heave ho," "uncovering buried treasure," or "all meals on deck."

If you checked six or more items, your child is quickly becoming a pirate—a sickly, injured pirate but a pirate nonetheless.

Your Pirate's First ship—
How to Convert Your Minivan
into a Pirate Schooner

Cap'n Billy always says, "A pirate without a ship is like a buccaneer without a boat." His point is that without a ship, a pirate is just a pathetic landlubber with an eye patch. But you may not live near the ocean or have the time to spend teaching your pirate to sail. Cap'n Billy's solution is to convert your minivan into a pirate schooner—a land-based pirate training vehicle!

You already spend way too much time driving your kids around town in your minivan. After your minivan is converted, your drive time can be wisely spent on naval training and the commute to your son's soccer game becomes a 15-minute exercise in ship navigation or artillery practice.

Common questions from parents

Isn't it expensive to convert a minivan into a pirate schooner?

Converting your minivan into a pirate schooner isn't as expensive as you'd think. And consider the cost of NOT converting your minivan into a pirate schooner. Your pirate won't even gain experience being a cabin boy because you have no cabin. You can find everything you need to convert your minivan at the local junkyard and army surplus store. Here are some items to put on your list:

- Flagpole to use as a mast
- Old barrel to use as crow's nest
- A swivel cannon that can handle a six-pound powder charge and is capable of penetrating two feet into solid wood at a range of 500 yards
- First aid kit

How do I convert my minivan?

If the minivan doesn't have a sunroof, make one using a chain saw or small explosive charge. This is the hatch from the cabin to the roof, which is now the main deck. Install the flagpole through the roof making sure to bolt it to the frame of the undercarriage. Reinforce the roof with ½-inch steel plates so it can hold a crew and the cannon. Install the cannon in the stern of the main deck.

Remove all seats from the inside of your van because the cab is now the cabin and cargo hold. You'll need plenty of space for rations, powder, cannon balls, casks of rum, and other items necessary for sailing around town.

Finding sails for your schooner is often the most difficult task. Sewing together bed sheets may seem like a good idea but sheets are too thin and rip easily. Cap'n Billy recommends Tyvek, a synthetic material made by DuPont. Tyvek is lightweight yet strong enough for sails. The most common uses for Tyvek are mailing envelopes and housewrap (the stuff wrapped around a house during construction to keep water out.) To get enough Tyvek to make your sails, either raid your local post office or visit a housing development that is under construction. If you opt for the mailing envelopes, you'll have a lot of sewing ahead of you. Housewrap is much larger, which is why Cap'n Billy calls it "sails on a roll."

Finally, make a pirate flag out of an old pillow case and fly it at the top of your mast. You're set to sail! If there's a strong enough wind, put your minivan in neutral and raise your sail. If it's a calm day, start your engine. Either way, you'll be the envy of all your friends and your pirate will gain valuable experience aboard ship.

While a more expensive option, a used microwave truck (the kind used by television news crews) makes the perfect pirate schooner. Microwave trucks have a retractable pole with a satellite dish that can extend more than 30 feet in the air. You don't even need to remove the satellite dish from the top of the pole before using it as a retractable mast! Without a retractable mast, you'll find your ability to pass through car washes and tunnels extremely limited.

I want to buy a new minivan but hate their names. What self-respecting pirate would drive something called Chrysler Town & Country?

Cap'n Billy shares your pain. During the past year, he has written to all the major minivan manufacturers and suggested new names for their products so they'd be more appealing to pirate families. The captain's suggestions include:

Old name

Buick Terraza

New name

Buick Black Squall

Chevrolet Uplander	*Chevy Me Timbers*
Chrysler Town & Country	*Chrysler Crow's Nest*
Dodge Caravan	*Dodge Deep Six*
Ford Freestar	*Ford Fishmonger*
Honda Odyssey	*Honda Hornswaggle*
Mazda MPV	*Mazda Mutiny*
Mercury Monterey	*Mercury Mizzen Mast*
Nissan Quest	*Nissan Neap Tide*
Pontiac Montana SV6	*Pontiac Poop Deck*
Saturn Relay	*Saturn Scurvy Scupper*
Toyota Sienna	*Toyota Tide Turner*

So far, Cap'n Billy has received only one response and that was a restraining order.

When I buy a new minivan, are there certain options that will come in handy once I've converted the vehicle into a pirate schooner?

Cap'n Billy has found that some options are more useful than others. For example, the captain doesn't see the need for doors on a minivan. But there are two options he always insists upon: Stow 'n Blow Seating and Bucket o' Chum Seats. Stow 'n Blow rear seats fold into the floor, allowing room for an internal, stern-mounted cannon. Just remember to open the rear door before firing (if you didn't remove the door entirely.) Bucket o' Chum seats are similar to bucket seats but are pretreated with a thick coat of oily fish. Finally, Cap'n Billy likes the feel of a wooden ship's wheel instead of the standard steering wheel.

We've converted our minivan into a pirate vessel but haven't named the ship yet. How does one go about naming a pirate ship?

Naming your pirate minivan is an important family activity and shouldn't be left to chance. So get a pair of dice and roll them. Use the chart below to find the first word in the name of your ship. Then roll the dice again to find the second word in the name of your ship.

Score	First word	Second word
2	*Plundering*	*Terror*
3	*Pillaging*	*Curse*
4	*Cruel*	*Ghost*
5	*Elusive*	*Plunderer*
6	*Drunken*	*Pillager*
7	*Burning*	*Snorter*
8	*Really, Really Mean*	*Squid*

9	*Festering*	*Shark*
10	*Bloody*	*Guppy*
11	*Blind*	*Derelict*
12	*Happy*	*Gollywobbler*

Feel free to roll the dice again if you're not satisfied with the name for your ship. *The Happy Guppy* won't instill terror but *The Bloody Terror* will. Some families like to add their name to their ship, so *The Drunken Pillager* becomes *The Johnson's Drunken Pillager*. This makes it easier to find your ship in a crowded parking lot and also reduces confusion when all your neighbors also name their pirate minivans *The Drunken Pillager*.

Is it okay to use a replica cannon on my ship?

"Only if you're training your child to be a 'pretend pirate,'" says Cap'n Billy. Get a grip and some real gunpowder.

What is the fewest number of crew members I need to sail my minivan?

Because the steering wheel is below the main deck, you need two pirates to sail your minivan—one to steer and one to man the sails and cannon. If you have cruise control, however, you can sail the vessel yourself. Just set the cruise control to the desired speed, crawl through the hatch to the main deck and enjoy the ride!

What's the best way to teach my pirate to sail the minivan?

Cap'n Billy has always been an advocate of the trial and error method. Whenever he's been on trial, he's told the judge, "There must be some error." This method will work for your pirate, too. At first your pirate may sail through a few lawns, shopping malls, and apartment complexes, but that's part of the freedom of being a pirate. No one tells a pirate where he can or can't sail. Besides, as long as your cannon is working, you won't get many complaints.

What can I fire from my cannon?

Cap'n Billy says you should pick your projectile based on your intent. Round shot (i.e., a large cannon ball) is used to put big holes in other ships. Chain shot (i.e., two smaller balls connected by chain) is perfect for ripping the sails of another ship. At times, you'll want to inflict terror without any physical or material damage. Mini-vans are usually loaded with the things your kids leave behind (e.g., kid's meal prizes, stale french fries, shoes, socks, balls, books, breakfast cereal). Cap'n Billy calls this "clean-the-car shot." Cram all the trash, toys, and so on into your cannon and fire them onto the lawn of the guy down the street who refuses to return the power drill he borrowed from you a year ago.

Cap'n Billy seems a little bit obsessed with cannons. Are all pirates like that?

Cannons include three things all pirates love: fire, loud noises, and destruction. (And the ability to repeat them until someone surrenders.)

My pirate asked me some questions about sailing that I've been unable to answer. Please help.

Question 1: *My pirate comes to a four-way stop and three other ships arrive at the exact same time my pirate does. Who has the right-of-way to enter the intersection first?*

Cap'n Billy isn't fond of stop signs and ignores them. But, usually, the right of way is given to ships in this order:

- 12-gun galleon
- 8-gun man of war
- 4-gun ketch

- Single-gun converted minivan

Unless Cap'n Billy is in the single-gun converted mini-van. Then he gets the right-of-way based on reputation.

Question 2: *My pirate is sailing and comes upon a school bus in his lane. The school bus is stopped with red lights flashing. What should my pirate do?*

Sail up alongside the bus and yell, "Don't waste yer time at school, maties, join me crew and learn the ways of the world!" This is an excellent way to quickly build a crew.

Question 3: *My pirate is approaching a railroad crossing and sees a train coming down the track. How should my pirate proceed?*

If it is a freight train with valuable cargo, Cap'n Billy recommends sailing alongside the train to board it. He's often been able to get a carload full of new automobiles or big screen TVs. If it's a commuter train, it's best to leave it alone. The only booty your pirate is likely to get is some old newspapers and empty coffee cups.

I want to teach my pirate how to keelhaul someone, but I'm not sure how to do it since my minivan doesn't have a keel. What do you suggest?

Keelhauling is the process of tying a person's hands with one long rope and his feet with another. One rope goes under the ship and the person is dragged or hauled underneath the ship until he comes out the other side. The purpose of keelhauling is to teach someone "not to go near Cap'n Billy's private stash of rum again." Because a ship's keel is covered with sharp barnacles, being keelhauled is a painful experience. It also requires holding one's breath for an extended period of time.

When discipline is required on your minivan, Cap'n Billy suggests "mufflerhauling." Mufflerhauling is similar to keelhauling except that the perpetrator is pulled across your schooner's hot muffler and, if he doesn't keep his mouth shut, may end up with a belly full of road kill. Like keelhauling, mufflerhauling requires the perpetrator to hold his breath — at least if there's a dead skunk in the road.

I'm a truck driver and have my own 18-wheeler. Can I convert that into a larger pirate ship?

Absolutely! The process for converting a larger truck is similar to the minivan conversion except that you'll need two additional masts, 12 additional cannons, and a crew of 20.

Has Cap'n Billy written any nursery rhymes about sailing the high seas?

Not only has he written them, he's lived them! Read these to your pirates-in-training:

Old Cap'n Rackham (Little Miss Muffet)

Old Cap'n Rackham left port for Siam,

Sailing the ocean blue.

Along came a maelstrom,

On an isle shipwrecked him,

And cannibals ate pirate stew.

Captain Had A Little Ship
(Mary Had A Little Lamb)

Captain had a little ship, its sails were white as sand,

And everywhere he sailed the ship,

    he tried to avoid land.

He sailed it to the keys one day, but landed on a reef,

Too bad he hadn't AAA,

    it would have saved some grief.

Captain waited patiently for the tide to flip,

Finally the tide came in and lifted up his ship.

"I hate the land," the captain said,

"That much I can't deny."

"And it hates you, tis true, tis true,"

his filthy crew replied.

Hey Piddle Piddle (Hey Diddle Diddle)

Hey piddle piddle, the pirate spat spittle,

To manners he was immune.

All day he drank rum and shot his gun,

Until he was sunk by a typhoon.

Cap'n Billy's land schooner sailing tips

Ignore traffic lights

Cap'n Billy finds traffic lights annoying, but they do provide a useful function—they tell you whether you're still on the road. Use traffic lights like sailors at sea use lighthouses. The light tells your approximate location but not whether you have to stop.

Convert mph to knots

Your pirate may be confused about the difference between miles per hour and knots (nautical miles per hour). To calculate the speed limit in knots, multiply it by 1.6. For example, a 55 mile per hour speed limit is 88 knots. If your pirate is ever pulled over for speeding, he should tell the officer how fast he was going in knots. If the officer doesn't understand how to convert knots to miles per hour, tell the officer to call the Coast Guard.

Don't study navigation

There are two schools of thought regarding the knowledge necessary to navigate a ship. The first is to spend years studying the ocean and weather patterns of the Atlantic, Pacific, and any other oceans in which you plan to sail. The second option, which is Cap'n Billy's preference, is to have OnStar installed in your ship. When your pirate pushes the OnStar button, a pleasant operator will tell him where he is located, as well as the locations of the closest merchant ships loaded with gold.

Your pirate's progress

Cap'n Billy loves bumper stickers because they allow him to preach his pirate philosophy to other people. He even puts stickers on the back of his ship. If your child has put an appropriate bumper stick on your pirate minivan, it's an indication that he is ready to sail without an adult on board. Please check off each bumper sticker your child has placed on your pirate minivan in the last six months.

☐ Rum: It's not just for breakfast anymore.

☐ Is my sailing bad? Call 1-800-PREPARE-TO-BE-BOARDED.

☐ Caution: I brake for buried treasure.

☐ Don't blame me, I'm from the Dry Tortugas.

☐ My other ship is an aircraft carrier.

☐ God must love stupid landlubbers, he made so many of them.

☐ I do whatever my parrot tells me.

☐ Become a pirate, meet interesting people, and plunder 'em.

☐ Back off! This ship is protected by a half-ton cannon and an ornery pirate.

☐ My pirate kidnapped your honor student.

☐ My dog's scurvy, but I still love him.

☐ I killed a bottle of rum just to watch it die.

If you checked two or more bumper stickers, your pirate has adopted the perfect pirate philosophy of life! Give him the keys to the pirate minivan and let him sail alone.

As Your Pirate Gets Older (The Teen Years and Beyond)

⌐∿⌐

The teenage years can be an adventure for parents—a nauseating, traumatizing adventure. As your pirate enters the teen years, he may experience erratic or emotionally unstable behavior and/or behavior that is disrespectful or defiant. It won't be long until your pirate turns this behavior away from you and toward his first crew. Congratulations! Before you know it, you'll be an "empty nester," or as Cap'n Billy likes to call it, an "empty crow's nester."

Common questions from parents

My daughter is asking for more independence but I don't know if I'm ready to let go yet. Is there a way to balance both of our needs?

Try setting limits you can both agree upon. If your daughter says she's going out with friends, decide where she is allowed to go and for how long. For example, "You can't leave the Atlantic Ocean and must be back within three months."

I want my teenager to be a pirate but he's become obsessed with becoming a ninja. What can I do?

Cap'n Billy suggests trying to reason with your son. Make a list of the pros and cons of being a ninja or a pirate.

Clothing

Ninjas wear black.

Pirates wear whatever they want, especially colorful outfits.

Language

Ninjas don't speak clearly or speak in Japanese with subtitles.

Pirates have trouble with their Rs but otherwise speak clearly when sober.

Punishment

Ninjas commit seppuku (i.e., suicide) when disgraced.

Pirates drink rum until they forget why they were disgraced.

Face coverings

Ninjas cover entire face—except eyes—with black cloth

Pirates cover eyes—but not face—with black cloth.

Killing

Ninjas kill others silently.

Pirates yell, "To Davy Jones's locker, ye scurvy bilge rat" when killing others.

Friends

Ninjas live a solitary lifestyle.

Pirates live with a great bunch of other pirates.

Food

Ninjas eat sushi (i.e., raw fish), which tastes awful.

Pirates eat salt cod (i.e., salt cod), which tastes awful.

After reviewing the lists, have a heart-to-heart discussion with your son about his decision to become a ninja. If he persists in his colossal ignorance, tell him you didn't spend 15 years of your life and $12.95 on this book to watch him flush his life down the toilet.

I don't think my teenager knows the difference between right and wrong. How can I help him understand this critical moral concept?

Cap'n Billy says that the difference between right and wrong is like the difference between plundering and pillaging. Plundering is taking goods that don't belong to you by force (e.g., Cap'n Billy *plundered* the merchant vessel and enjoyed the chests of gold he took). Pillaging, on the other hand, is taking goods that don't belong to you by force (e.g., Cap'n Billy *pillaged* the merchant vessel and enjoyed the chests of gold he took). Pirates excel in both activities and can't tell the two apart. Nor can they tell the difference between right and wrong.

My pirate is shy and hasn't dated much. How can I help him come out of his shell?

Cap'n Billy learned the hard way that the pick-up line, "Wench, bring me another drink," isn't very effective, unless you want the drink thrown at you. Cap'n Billy believes online dating is the best way to meet new people because it allows a pirate to control the first impression others have of him. (Surprisingly, some people don't find missing teeth and eyes attractive.)

Have your teen carefully consider what he includes in his online dating profile. Below is how Cap'n Billy translated his personal information:

Name:

The truth: Cap'n Billy "The Butcher" MacDougall

Translated for dating profile: William MacDougall

Occupation:

The truth: Pirate captain

Translated for dating profile: Freelance naval consultant and philanthropist

Hair:

The truth: Dark, thick, and greasy (especially on me back)

Translated for dating profile: Black

Eyes:

The truth: One real; one glass

Translated for dating profile: Brown

Looks:

The truth: A little like Danny DeVito, if he were much taller and missing some teeth

Translated for dating profile: Stunningly handsome with a military air

Build:

The truth: Cannons, chests, and anything else I need for me ship

Translated for dating profile: Athletic

Hobbies:

The truth: Smoking, drinking, digging for buried treasure, attacking merchant ships, and pilfering other people's property

Translated for dating profile: Socializing, walks on the beach, sailing, and helping others

Favorite cultural activity:

The truth: A night I can remember the next morning

Translated for dating profile: A night at the opera

Favorite movie:

The truth: I've watched *Pirates of the Caribbean* more than 600 times

Translated for dating profile: Pride and Prejudice or anything else based on a Jane Austin novel

I can't get my teenager to do anything around the house. She's messy and often rude. Any suggestions?

Cap'n Billy suggests promoting her to corporal. She's obviously officer material.

My teenager doesn't listen to me. What can I do?

Many teenagers say they "hear voices" but can't understand what "the voices" are saying. These teenagers may seek psychiatric help because they think they are going crazy when, in fact, they have simply tuned out their parents to such an extent that their parents' voices sound like babbling in the distance. Before you speak to your pirate, make sure he is looking you in the eye. Then hit your pirate in the head with an oar. This won't help your pirate hear, but it will make you feel a lot better.

My teen is going through difficult emotional changes. How can I help?

In 1956, psychiatrist Erik Erikson created his famous theory of the "Eight Stages of Social-Emotional Development," in which he described how people struggle between alternatives during their lives (e.g., trust vs. mistrust, autonomy vs. shame, intimacy vs. isolation.) Unfortunately, Erikson's theory is a bunch of rubbish and is no help in raising a teenage pirate. That's why

Cap'n Billy created his not-so-famous theory of the "Pieces-of-eight Stages of Pirate Social-Emotional Development," in which he describes how pirates struggle between difficult choices during different stages of their lives.

Stage 1: Cloth or disposable? When it comes to diapers, Cap'n Billy recommends disposal ones. Sure they take up a huge amount of space in landfills, but pirates don't spend that much time on land.

Stage 2: Barney or SpongeBob SquarePants? While you might expect SpongeBob to win out, Cap'n Billy thinks Barney would be more valuable in a fight. Barney is big enough to hide behind and could be used as a life raft in an pinch.

Stage 3: Frosted Flakes or Cap'n Crunch? Although Cap'n Crunch isn't a pirate, he is still respected by pirates for his love of the sea and for the invention of Crunch Berries.

Stage 4: Coke or Pepsi? Cap'n Billy prefers Pepsi. He hates anything people mix with rum because it "waters it down."

Stage 5: New England or Manhattan Clam Chowder? After spending six months at sea, Cap'n Billy prefers Beef and Barley Soup to anything with clams in it.

Stage 6: The Who or The Rolling Stones? This one's a draw for Cap'n Billy. While he knows he can't always get what he wants, he also realizes he can see for miles (and miles) when he's up in the crow's nest.

Stage 7: Paper or plastic? The choice really depends on what you're buying. Cannon balls fit better in a plastic bag, but cans of sea rations are better held in a paper bag.

Stage 8: Cabernet Sauvignon or Petit Sirah? While pirates prefer rum, Cap'n Billy has been known to partake in a glass of Petit Sirah now and again. He likes Petit Sirah because, if you rearrange the letters, it spells "Pirates hit" or "a heist trip." When you rearrange the letters of "Cabernet Sauvignon," all you get is "A beavers con gun nit."

Cap'n Billy's theory is fascinating, but it doesn't answer how I can help my teenager cope with emotional changes?

Get your teen a pet parrot and tell him to get over it.

How can my teen resist peer pressure?

Peer pressure isn't only common among teens, it's also common among pirates. How else can you explain how Cap'n Billy was able to goad another pirate into having "I'm one shrimp short of a combo platter" tattooed on his forehead.

When one of your teen's peers pressures him to do something he doesn't want to do, instruct your teen to do the following:

1) *Firmly and calmly say "no."*

2) *If that doesn't work, firmly and calmly tell the friend to "walk the plank because all the cool pirates are doing it."*

3) *If that doesn't work, firmly and calmly push the friend overboard.*

I want my pirate to have great role models. Who would you say was the greatest pirate of all time?

Many people think it was Willie Stargell, who hit 475 home runs for the Pittsburgh Pirates between 1962 and 1982. Others would vote for Bill Mazeroski, who had a .983 career fielding percentage. But the greatest pirate of all time was actually "Inky" Tom Smythe, who in 1897 ate a dozen squid on a dare and then burped four verses of "Blow the Man Down."

My teen is illegally downloading music from the Internet. What should I do?

Tell your teen that becoming a "software pirate" is not the same thing as becoming a swashbuckler of the high seas. Software pirates tend to be loners who like to steal things without actually confronting the person from whom they are stealing. Real pirates appreciate the joy of seeing the terror on other people's faces when they are being pillaged.

What's a good first job for my pirate?

Your teen's first job is a critical step in becoming a fully independent pirate. The most common first job for teenagers is working at a fast-food restaurant. These restaurants are good places to practice taking orders and even giving a few. Cap'n Billy suggests helping your teen get a job working the drive-thru window, where he can illustrate competence that will ensure his promotion to the day shift! Here are some great pirate responses for your teen to use while at work to show his management potential:

• "Please sail up to the first window so I can plunder yer wallet."

• "Would you like to be the first person to try our new tentacle burger? It's squid legs between two stale pieces of hardtack."

- "Yes, you can pay in pennies, as long as I can flog you with french fries."
- "We can't take your order right now. We're busy planning a mutiny."
- "Give me your car keys, matey, you're too dumb to drive," when asked questions, such as, "How many pieces are in the eight-piece chicken nuggets."

My pirate is very interested in piercings, but I'm concerned that he will get too many. How can we compromise?

Cap'n Billy knows many pirates for whom piercings got out of hand. Piercings are especially hazardous if your pirate falls overboard and is dragged to the bottom of the sea by the weight of his rings, chains, and other permanent bling.

Have your teen jump into a swimming pool with a small anchor tied to his feet. If he's able to swim for 60 minutes with the weight, then set the limit of his jewelry as the anchor weight. If your teen sinks to the bottom of the pool, use a slightly lighter anchor and try again until you find the appropriate weight for his rings and things.

Cap'n Billy's teenage pirate training tips

Use "aye" statements rather than "you" statements.

Your teen will act defensive if you say things such as, "You best clean up your room, if ye know what's good for you, me hearty." On the other hand, if you use an "aye" statement, you'll have better luck. For example, "If ye don't say 'aye, aye, sir,' when I ask ye to clean your room, you'll be scrubbing the scuppers with your toothbrush."

Volunteer together

Working together is a great way to connect with your teen.

Visit a home for elderly pirates and help them furl their sails or find their misplaced hooks, legs, teeth, and so on.

Be positive

Root for your pirate whenever possible. Show up when your teen is in a school play, sports activity, or naval skirmish. Be the parent in the front row who claps loudly and shouts, "That's me pirate!"

Give your teenager space

Sometimes its useful to get an ocean between you

and your pirate. Wait until your pirate is sleeping soundly, and then put him on a slow boat to China or any other distant port. By the time he gets back, you'll both feel better about yourselves.

Respect your pirate's privacy

When you rummage through your pirate's room and sell his prized-possessions on e-Bay, offer to give your teen 10 percent of the net profits.

Your pirate's progress

According to Cap'n Billy, there are ten signs that your child is ready to venture out on his or her own. Please check off each sign that your child has exhibited in the last three months.

☐ Your teen's cell phone ringtone is a sea shanty.

☐ Your teen complains that his allowance isn't high enough to pay for "lavish pirate lifestyle."

☐ Your teen gets misty-eyed when watching *Pirates of the Caribbean* movies.

☐ Your teen has already put a crew together, and they're spending way too much time watching TV in your basement and eating your food.

❏ A high school aptitude test showed your teen has a great talent for high treason and skullduggery.

❏ Your teen's college entrance application essay that compared university professors to "drunken parrots with computers" didn't impress any schools.

❏ Your child is already wanted in 16 states and three oceans.

❏ Your child finally finished patching the holes in the hull of the 100-foot schooner that's been on blocks in your back yard for six years.

❏ Cap'n Billy asked your teen to join his crew.

❏ You recently changed the locks on your doors and didn't want to spend the extra $1.29 for a key for your teen.

If you checked six or more items, your teen is ready to set sail alone. Fill a duffle bag with his personal belongings and leave it on your front steps.

Congratulations! You've Completed Captain Billy "The Butcher" MacDougall's Guide to Pirate Parenting!

If you found this book useful, keep on the lookout for these future titles from Cap'n Billy:

- *I'm Okay, You're a Stinking, Scurvy Landlubber: Using Transactional Analysis to Unleash Your Inner Pirate*
- *The Marooner's Diet: How You Can Lose 90 pounds by Spending a Month Stranded on an Island*
- *Cap'n Billy's Guide to Rum-based Cocktails for Every Occasion*
- *Brotherhood of the Traveling Eye Patch*
- *The World Is Flat, but I Can Still Plunder It: A Brief Pirate History of the Twenty-first Century*
- *The Five People You Meet During a Pub Crawl*
- *Cap'n Billy's Ship keeping Handbook: The Essential Guide to Caring for Everything in Your Schooner (includes hints for getting gun power and blood stains out of your fine linen)*

Do you have questions not answered in this book? Ask Cap'n Billy at www.PirateParenting.com!

About the Authors

Tim Bete (pronounced "beet") began his nautical adventures as a child sailing on Buzzards Bay off the coast of Massachusetts. At age ten, he longed for a small cannon to put on his grandfather's 30-foot wooden ketch—a quick, two-masted vessel that is perfect for catching other ships so you can plunder 'em. His parents scuttled the cannon idea, saying he "would terrorize other boats with it." That's exactly what he had in mind.

Bete's parenting advice has been published in dozens of newspapers, magazines, and Web sites, including *The Christian Science Monitor, Atlanta Parent, Big Apple Parent, Northwest Family,* Fathers World.com, and ParentingHumor.com. His first book, *In the Beginning…There Were No Diapers,* was a 2006 *ForeWord* Best Book of the Year finalist.

Bete's hobbies include pushing his luck and skating on thin ice. He's the former director of the Erma Bombeck Writers' Workshop (www.HumorWriters.org).

Cap'n Billy "The Butcher" MacDougall (pronounced "MacDougall") has been hiding from authorities for most of his life. He lives on his ship, *The Frightened Flounder,* but can sometimes be found at the *Crow's Nest Tavern*. His hobbies include plundering and rum.

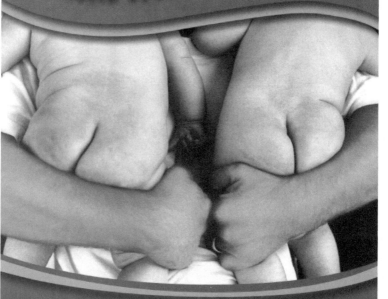

In The Beginning...
THERE WERE NO DIAPERS

Laughing and Learning
In the First Years of Fatherhood

TIM BETE

Also by Tim Bete...
In the Beginning...There Were No Diapers

~

"...irreverent, clever and incredibly reassuring...Bete offers up his personal, hilarious research that will make your foray into parenting seem like a walk along the beach."
—*ePregnancy Magazine*

"Tim Bete is the Dave Barry for parents of young kids..."
—Heather Ivester, editor, *Mom 2 Mom Connection*

"Smart, clever and funny.
I laughed out loud at least once on every page."
—Karyl Miller, Emmy award-winning sitcom writer-producer whose credits include *The Cosby Show* and *The Mary Tyler Moore Show*.

"Elicits laughs, chuckles and smiles with the same good-natured, self-deprecating approach that made Bombeck the patron saint of frazzled mothers."
—*Stamford Advocate*

Get your copy of *In the Beginning...There Were No Diapers* at www.TimBete.com.